Very Simple

ARABIC
SCRIPT

Very Simple

ARABIC SCRIPT

Written and illustrated

by

James Peters

STACEY INTERNATIONAL

VERY SIMPLE ARABIC SCRIPT

Published by
Stacey International
128 Kensington Church Street
London W8 4BH
Tel: 0207 221 7166; Fax: 0207 792 9288
E-mail: marketing@stacey-international.co.uk
Website: www.stacey-international.co.uk

© Stacey International & James Peters 2003
Reprinted 2004

3 5 7 9 8 6 4 2

ISBN: 1 900988 313

Printed & bound by Times Offset (M) Sdn.Bhd.

British Library Catalogue in Publication Data:
A catalogue record for this book is available from
the British Library.

Front cover illustration: *'ahlan wa sahlan'* – a traditional
Arab greeting meaning 'Welcome!'

Introduction

One of the reasons Arabic is considered a difficult language to learn is the daunting appearance of the script. However, it is not as complicated as it looks and my aim in this book is to explain it in the simplest of terms, enabling visitors to the Arab world to read the words, notices and signs they see around them and know how they sound. The book is also intended to be comprehensive enough to provide a good grounding for serious students of the language.

A knowledge of the script is generally regarded as the key to a proper understanding of the Arabic language, and a basic grammar and vocabulary have been included for those who wish to make a start in that direction.

Allow yourself time to absorb the information. The explanations of the letters and the script are designed to be read in sequence and, given time, will result in a clear understanding of the Arabic writing system.

JAMES PETERS

Acknowledgements

I am especially indebted to Sir John Wilton KCMG, KCVO, MC, Dr Paul Starkey, Lawrie Walker, Christopher Wilton, Richard Palmer, Max Scott and Kitty Carruthers for their kind advice on the manuscript of this book. However, responsibility for the content is mine alone.

J.P.

Contents

A Note on the Transliteration of Arabic Words and Pronunciation

The transliteration of Arabic words into English (*given in italics*) has been kept as simple as possible and words should be pronounced as the English spelling suggests.

Although any written guide to pronunciation will have its limitations, the pronunication of Arabic is greatly simplified by the fact that it is a phonetic language – words are pronounced exactly as they are written. There are no silent letters, as in English.

Where necessary, the stress syllable is shown in bold type.

Although most beginners are naturally shy about pronouncing words which are strange to them, do not be put off. It does not matter if you sound a little odd as Arabs are used to hearing a variety of accents from within the Arab world and will generally be delighted that you have made the effort. Do not take correction as criticism - it will improve your fluency and help establish a rapport.

The Arabic Language

The Arabic language is used throughout the Arab world by more than 120 million people and is the religious language of another 700 to 800 million Muslims in 60 non-Arab countries. The script is also used with modifications in Farsi (Persian), Urdu and Kurdish.

The language is enshrined in the Holy Quran, which is the record of the message revealed by the Archangel Gabriel to the Prophet Muhammad. It is important to realise that for this reason Arabic is revered by Muslims as sacred – the 'language of God'. Classical Arabic, derived from the Holy Quran, is rich in its vocabulary, breadth of description, hyperbole, metaphor, rhyme and rhythm. When reciting from the Holy Quran, in poetry or in prose, together with its precisely inflected vowels, Arabs find the literary eloquence and power of expression of the language intensely moving.

Spoken Arabic varies from country to country, each having its own dialect, but written Arabic is based on the classical language and is the same throughout the Arab world.

This written language, often referred to as 'modern standard Arabic' or 'modern literary Arabic', is used in newspapers, books, public notices and in radio and television broadcasts.

It is the script based on 'modern standard Arabic' which is explained in this book.

Finally, a knowledge of the script is generally regarded as the key to a proper understanding of the Arabic language.

2
The Arabic Script

The principal characteristics of the Arabic script are briefly as follows:

◆ It is written from right to left and a book or magazine in Arabic opens at the opposite end to one in English.

◆ The alphabet has 28 letters with an additional special sign which largely functions as a letter.

◆ Letters change shape with their position in a word (depending on whether they come at the beginning, middle or end) but they all have a basic characteristic that makes them clearly recognisable wherever they appear. When the writing system is understood, these changes in shape are seen as perfectly logical.

◆ The script is cursive, which means that most of the letters join together, in both hand-written and printed text. In fact, all the letters can be joined to a preceding letter but six of them have the peculiarity that they cannot be joined to a following one. These six are called 'non-connecting' letters.

- There are only three vowels in Arabic, each with a short and a long version:

  - Short vowels are written as small marks above or below the consonants but are not shown in modern text.

  - Long vowels are formed by combining the short vowels with three of the letters of the alphabet.

- There are no capital letters in Arabic.

- Most of the letters have an equivalent sound in English. However, the pronunciation of Arabic is simplified by the fact that it is phonetic and, unlike English, words are pronounced exactly as they are written.

One characteristic of the script which often puzzles the newcomer to Arabic is the varying thickness of the letters. This attractive feature derives from the time when the early Islamic calligraphers wrote with pens usually fashioned from a reed.

The size and shape of the nib of the reed,
normally cut at an angle as illustrated below,
determined the calligraphic style. This
characteristic has been preserved in modern
printed styles and explains why Arabic letters,
written from the top generally in a clockwise
motion, vary in thickness and why the dots in
the script are diamond-shaped.

These variations in thickness do not make the
script any more difficult to read since the
basic shape of each letter is always
recognisable – as will become clear in the
next chapter.

REED PEN

The Letters of the Alphabet

Sequence reading from left to right

ا	ب	ت	ث	ج	ح	خ
'alif	baa'	taa'	thaa'	jeem	_h_aa'	khaa'

د	ذ	ر	ز	س	ش	ص
daal	dhaal	raa'	_z_aa'	seen	sheen	_s_aad

ض	ط	ظ	ع	غ	ف	ق
_d_aad	_t_aa'	_dh_aa'	ayn	ghayn	faa'	qaaf

ك	ل	م	ن	ه	و	ي
kaaf	laam	meem	noon	haa'	waaw	yaa'

Special sign ء *hamza*

3

The Arabic Alphabet

This chapter describes the vowels and other signs used to indicate pronunciation, followed by an explanation of each letter of the alphabet.

The three short vowels in Arabic are:

fatha   —   A short diagonal stroke written above a consonant, usually pronounced like the 'a' in 'pat'. Transliterated as *a*.

damma   —   A small sign resembling a comma written above a consonant and pronounced like the 'u' in 'put'. Transliterated as *u*.

kasra   —   A short diagonal stroke written below a consonant and pronounced like the 'i' in 'bit'. Transliterated as *i*.

When a consonant does not have a vowel, a tiny circle is placed above it. This sign is called a *sukoon*:   ◎

Double consonants in Arabic are not written twice
as in English but a small sign like a 'w' is put
above them indicating that they are doubled:

This sign is called a *shadda* and a consonant
with a *shadda* is pronounced twice. The process
of doubling is called *tashdeed* which means
'strengthening' in Arabic.

When a *shadda* is combined with a short vowel
over a consonant, the *fatha* and the *damma* are
written above the *shadda*:

and the *kasra* is either written below the *shadda*
or beneath the letter itself:

either   or

Although the short vowels and other signs are
always written in the Holy Quran and other
classical literary works, they are normally
omitted in modern written Arabic.

Exceptionally, one sign that is included in
modern text is a double *fatha* ✔ written at the
end of some words (for example, the words on
the cover of this book) which has a special
grammatical function and is pronounced '*an*'.
This is fully explained in the next chapter.

'alif

The first letter of the alphabet is *'alif* which is illustrated above in what is termed the 'stand-alone' form. It is basically a vertical line.

'alif is one of the six letters previously mentioned (on page 3) as 'non-connecting' *i.e.* it cannot be connected to a following letter.

Therefore, when a word starts with an *'alif* there is a gap between it and the next letter.

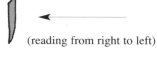

next letter   (reading from right to left)

In the middle of a word, however, where *'alif* can, like all the letters of the alphabet, be joined to a preceding letter, it appears:

next letter   join from the preceding letter

But if the *'alif* were preceded by another non-connecting letter, then it would have to appear in stand-alone form:

next letter   preceding non-connector

9

Finally, at the end of a word, connected to a preceding letter, *'alif* appears:

join from the preceding letter

but if preceded by another non-connector then it would again appear in the stand-alone form.

'alif is always recognisable by its basic characteristic as a vertical line, which can be joined to a preceding letter but never to a following one.

'alif is unique among the letters in having two major functions. At this point we will deal only with the first of these – the formation of the long 'a' vowel.*

Whenever a *fatha* short 'a' vowel is followed by an *'alif*, which is its associated letter, the combination makes a long 'a' vowel:

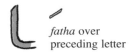

fatha over preceding letter

The long 'a' vowel

The long 'a' vowel is usually pronounced as the 'a' in 'father'. In certain combinations of letters it can also sound like the 'a' in 'ban' but this variation is pointed out whenever it occurs. In transliteration the long 'a' vowel is written *aa*.

* The second function is explained later on page 52.

The second letter of the alphabet is one of a family of three with a basic shape resembling a wide shallow boat. They are all 'connecting' letters. In the case of the *baa'* (above in stand-alone form) it has a dot below the boat in the centre.

At the beginning of a word only the front part of the *baa'* is written, connected to the following letter and the dot is placed beneath it:

In the middle of a word, *baa'* is written as a little hook connected to the letters before and after it and again with the dot underneath it:

At the end of a word, connected only to a letter before it, the complete shape of the *baa'* is written:

The distinctive dot written below the various shapes described above make the *baa'* readily recognisable anywhere in the script.

If, in the middle of a word, *baa'* appears after a non-connecting letter such as an *'alif*, then it takes the same form as at the beginning of a word:

and if a *baa'* appears after a non-connecting letter at the end of a word, again such as an *'alif*, then it takes the stand-alone form:

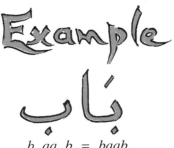

baa' is pronounced like the English 'b' and is transliterated as *b*.

Example

ب اب

b aa b = baab

In the above example the combination of the *fatha* and the *'alif* make a long 'a' vowel. The *'alif* can connect to a preceding letter but not a following one and therefore the final *baa'* is written in its stand-alone form.

This word is pronounced as the English word 'barb'. There is no word for 'a' or 'an' in Arabic and *baab* means 'a door' or 'a chapter'.

The next letter shares the same boat shape as the *baa'* and behaves in the same way but the *taa'*, illustrated above in its stand-alone form, has two dots above the boat.

At the beginning of a word *taa'* is written:

In the middle of a word:

and at the end of a word:

Like the *baa'*, if the *taa'* comes after a non-connecting letter in the middle or at the end of a word then it is written:

end of a word   middle of a word

The *taa'* is the only letter of the alphabet with two dots above a hook or a boat shape and this makes it easily recognisable.

The *taa'* is pronounced as the 't' in 'top' and is transliterated as *t*.

The final letter in the family is *thaa'* which has
three dots in a small triangle above the boat
shape. In its three forms, at the beginning, middle
and end of a word it is written:

| end | middle | beginning |

This triangle of three dots above a hook or a
boat shape is the characteristic feature of the
thaa' in the script.

thaa' is pronounced as 'th' in 'thing'. It is
transliterated in English as *th*.

In the example below a *thaa'* is followed by a *baa'*
and a *taa'*.

*th   a   b   a   t   a   =   **thabata***

All of the above letters can be connected to each
other and this word is pronounced as spelt in the
English transliteration ***thabata***. It is the Arabic
verb meaning 'to be firm' or 'stable'.

The next three letters are also a family with the same shape, the only difference between them being the placing of the dots. They are all connecting letters.

The first of the family is *jeem* illustrated in stand-alone form above. At the beginning of a word only the top part is written and connected to the following letter. The dot is placed underneath:

The same is true in the middle of a word but with connections from both the preceding letter and to the following one. The dot is again placed underneath. The line from the preceding letter may connect on top or bottom of the *jeem*:

At the end of a word, the complete shape of the *jeem* is written with a connecting line from the preceding letter and the dot inside the tail:

If, in the middle of a word a *jeem* is preceded by a non-connecting letter such as an *'alif*, then it takes the same form as at the beginning of a word:

If preceded by a non-connecting letter such as an *'alif* at the end of a word, the *jeem* is written in its stand-alone form:

In most of The Arab World *jeem* is pronounced as the 'j' in 'jet'.* It is transliterated as *j*.

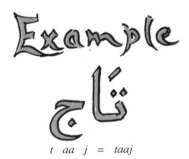

t   aa   j   =   taaj

The combination of the *fatha* and the *'alif* make a long 'a' vowel and because the *'alif* cannot be joined to a following letter the final *jeem* is written in its stand-alone form. Pronounced in English as *'tarj'* this is the word for 'a crown'.

* In the Levant the *jeem* is pronounced as the French 'je' but in Egypt and parts of Oman and Yemen as a hard 'g'.

The second letter in this family is <u>haa</u>'. It has the same shape as the *jeem* but no dot.

At the beginning of a word, as for *jeem*, it is written:

In the middle of a word:

   *or*

and at the end of a word:

and in the middle or at the end of a word preceded by a non-connecting letter such as '*alif*:

There are two letters with an 'h' sound. <u>haa</u>' is pronounced in a strongly aspirated way, like the emphatic 'h' in 'hit'. It is transliterated as <u>h</u>. The other 'h', described on page 45, is lighter, like a soft version of the 'h' in 'he' and transliterated as *h*.

The third letter in this family is *khaa'*. It has the same basic shape as the *jeem* and the *haa'* but in this case the dot is placed above the letter.

At the beginning, middle and end of a word it is written:

end   middle   beginning

The *khaa'* sounds like the 'ch' in the Scottish pronunciation of the word 'loch'. It is important to give the sound its full value to distinguish it from *haa'*. It is transliterated as *kh*.

Example

b a kh t = bakht

Note that all the letters are 'connectors'. The *sukoon* over the *khaa'* means that it is pronounced together with the *taa'*.

This word means 'luck' in Arabic.

The next two letters, *daal* and *dhaal* are a pair with exactly the same basic shape, the only distinction as usual being the dot. They are non-connectors *i.e.* they do not connect to a following letter.

At the start of a word, being non-connectors, they are written in their stand-alone form:

next letter   next letter

In the middle of a word, they can only be joined to a preceding letter and therefore are written:

next letter   next letter

and at the end of a word:

The *daal* is pronounced as the English letter 'd' and the *dhaal* like the hard 'th' in 'that'. (Note the distinction between the sound of this letter and the *thaa'* on page 14 which is pronounced as 'th' in 'thing'.)

daal is transliterated as *d* and *dhaal* as *dh*.

Examples

d a j aa j = da**jaaj**

The *daal* cannot be connected to the *jeem* which
is in the form it takes at the beginning of a word.
The combination of the *fatha* and the *'alif* make a
long 'a' vowel and the *'alif* cannot be connected
to the final *jeem* which is therefore in its stand-
alone form. Finally, note the stress syllable at the
end. This is the collective word for 'chickens' in
Arabic.

dh u b aa b = dhu**baab**

Note that the *dhaal* cannot be connected to the
first *baa'* which is therefore in the form it takes at
the beginning of a word. The combination of the
fatha and the *'alif* make a long 'a' vowel and the
'alif cannot be connected to the final *baa'* which
is therefore in stand-alone form. Finally, note the
stress syllable.

In this particular word the long 'a' vowel is
pronounced as the 'a' in 'ban' rather than the 'a'
in 'father'. (See page 10).

This is the collective word for 'flies' in Arabic.

The *raa'* and the *zaa'** are another pair with exactly the same shape, the only difference between them being the dot. They are non-connecting letters.

Their shape is differentiated from the *daal* and the *dhaal,* which have sharp angles, by having a smoother crescent shape and they extend below the line of writing (see examples below) rather than sitting on top of it.

At the start of a word, being non-connectors, the *raa'* and the *zaa'* are written in their stand-alone form:

next letter   next letter

In the middle of a word where they can be connected to a preceding letter but not a following one, they are written:

next letter   next letter

and at the end of a word, connected only to a preceding letter, they are written:

* sometimes called *zay.*

The *raa'* is pronounced as an English 'r' but is rolled. It is transliterated as *r*.

The zaa' is pronounced as the 'z' in 'zoo' and is transliterated as *z*.

r   aa   t   i   b = **raa**tib

The *raa'* cannot connect to a following letter and neither can the *'alif*. The *fatha* and the *'alif* make a long 'a' vowel. Finally, because the 'alif is a non-connector, the *taa'* takes the form it has at the beginning of a word. This is the Arabic word for 'a salary'.

z   u   j   aa   j = *zu**jaaj***

The *zaa'* cannot be connected to the *jeem* which is in the form it takes at the beginning of a word. The *fatha* and the *'alif* make a long 'a' vowel and the *'alif* cannot connect to the final *jeem* which is in stand-alone form.

This is the collective word in Arabic for 'glass'.

Here we should introduce the letter *waaw*, which although it is out of alphabetical sequence, is not only a consonant but makes the long 'u' vowel. It also has two other minor functions. It is the last of the six non-connecting letters.

At the beginning of a word, because it cannot connect to a following letter, it is written in the stand-alone form illustrated above:

next letter

In the middle and at the end of a word, connected to a preceding letter, it is written:

end ⟍⟍⟍   next letter ⟍⟍⟍ middle

When it is a consonant, the *waaw* is pronounced as the 'w' in 'wet' and is transliterated as *w*. As an example:

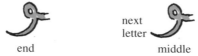

w   aa   <u>h</u>   i   d   = **waa<u>h</u>id**

Note that the waaw cannot connect to the *'alif*, *fatha* combined with *'alif* makes a long 'a' vowel and the *'alif* cannot connect to the *<u>haa</u>'*.

This is the Arabic word for 'one' (masc.).

The Long 'u' Vowel

Whenever a *damma* short vowel is followed by a *waaw*, its associated letter, the combination makes a long 'u' vowel.

The long 'u' vowel is pronounced 'oo' as in 'loop' and is transliterated as *oo*.

For example:

r oo h̲ = roo̲h̲

Neither the *raa'* nor the *waaw* can be joined to a following letter and therefore all the letters are written in stand-alone form. The combination of the *damma* and the *waaw* make a long 'u' vowel. This word means 'a spirit' or 'a soul' in Arabic.

Other Functions

Whenever a *fatha* is followed by a *waaw* with a *sukoon* the combination makes the diphthong *aw*:

d aw r = dawr

daal and *waaw* are both non-connectors and all the letters are therefore in stand-alone form. This word, *dawr*, pronounced as in the English 'dower', means 'a turn' or 'a period' in Arabic.

The final functions of the *waaw* are explained later in the book. (see pages 52 and 96).

The *seen* and the *sheen* are another pair with the same basic shape, the only difference between them being the triangle of three dots in the case of the *sheen*. Both are connecting letters.

At the beginning of a word, connected to a following letter, only the group of three little hooks at the front of the letter are written:

In the middle of a word the group of three little hooks is connected to the preceding and the following letters:

But at the end of a word, connected to a preceding letter, the full shape is written:

The *seen* and *sheen* are always recognisable by the distinctive group of three little hooks and in the case of the *sheen* by the three dots as well.

The *seen* is pronounced as the 's' in 'sip' and is transliterated as *s*. The *sheen* is pronounced as the 'sh' in 'sheep' and is transliterated as *sh*.

Examples

*s a b a b = **sabab***

As all the letters are connecting ones, this word
is straightforward in writing. It means 'a reason'
or 'a cause' in Arabic.

*r a sh sh aa sh = **rashshaash***

The *raa'* cannot be connected to the *sheen*
which is therefore written in the form it takes at
the beginning of a word. The combination of
the *fatha* and the *'alif* make a long 'a' vowel and,
because the *'alif* cannot be connected to a
following letter, the final *sheen* is written in
stand-alone form.

As explained on page 8, the *shadda* over the first
sheen means that it must be said twice, *i.e.* the
pronunciation of this word is emphasised as:

*rash-**shaash***

This means 'a machine gun' in Arabic.

These two letters are again identical, except for the dot, and are both connecting letters.

At the start of a word, connected to a following letter, only the loop with the hook is written:

In the middle of a word connected to both a preceding and a following letter it is the same:

and at the end of a word, connected only to a preceding letter, the full shape is written:

These letters are difficult for the beginner to pronounce at first. Together with the two letters that follow them in the alphabet they are known as the 'emphatic consonants'.

The _saad_ is an 'emphatic' form of the _seen_. The _seen_ is a light sound said from the front of the mouth, like the 's' in 'sip', but the _saad_ is much deeper and comes from the back. The *saad* is pronounced like the 'sw' in 'sword' but said more forcefully and shorter.

Similarly, *daad* is the emphatic form of *daal*. Whereas *daal* sounds like the 'd' in 'did', *daad* is pronounced deeper like the 'dau' in 'daunt' and said more forcefully and shorter.

These letters are transliterated as *s* and *d* and underlined to mark their 'emphatic' nature.

The *saad* and the *daad* affect the sound of the vowels around them, as illustrated in the following examples:

s a b aa h = sabaah

The combination of the *fatha* and the *'alif* make a long 'a' vowel. The sound of the *saad* affects the following *fatha* and results in this particular word actually being pronounced *as sobaah*. This means 'a morning' in Arabic.

d a r a b a = daraba

The sound of the *d* affects the following *fatha* and this particular word is pronounced *doroba,* which is the Arabic verb meaning 'to beat'.

These are the other two 'emphatic consonants' and are again identical, except for the dot. They are connecting letters.

The _taa'_ and the _dhaa'_ do not alter shape in writing. At the start of a word, connected to a following letter they are written:

Note that there is no hook after the loop as with the previous two letters, the _saad_ and the _daad_.

In the middle of a word, connected to both a preceding and a following letter, they are written:

and at the end of a word, connected only to a preceding letter:

The _taa'_ is the 'emphatic' form of the _taa'_ but whereas the _taa'_ is a light sound said from the front of the mouth, as the 't' in 'top', the _taa'_

is much deeper and comes from the back. _taa'_ sounds like the 'tau' in 'taught' but shorter and said more forcefully.

Similarly, the _dhaa'_ is the 'emphatic' form of the _dhaal_. The _dhaal_ sounds like the 'th' in 'then' but the _dhaa'_ is a deeper, more forceful version of it.*

The _taa'_ and the _dhaa'_ are transliterated as _t_ and _dh_ respectively, the underlining marking their 'emphatic' nature.

As with the other 'emphatic' letters, the _taa'_ and the _dhaa'_ usually affect the sound of the vowels around them, but in the two examples below this is minimal:

*kh a t a r = **khatar!***

A common sign in Arab countries on installations such as electricity substations, this means 'danger!' in Arabic.

_dh_ i rr = _dhirr_

This means 'a sharp edged stone' or 'a flint' in Arabic.

* _dhaa'_ can alternatively be pronounced as a deep 'z' sound; a forceful version of the 'zo' in 'zoro'.

As usual the only difference between these two letters is the dot. Both are connecting letters.

At the start of a word only the top part of the letter is written:

In the middle of a word, connected to a preceding and a following letter, they change shape completely:

At the end of a word, connected only to the preceding letter they have the same shape but with the tail:

Note the enclosed shape of the top of these letters in order to differentiate them from the *jeem* family (see page 15).

At the end of a word but after a non-connecting letter the complete stand-alone form illustrated at the top of the page would be written.

ع . غ

31

The sounds of these letters are among the most difficult to master as there is no equivalent in English.

The letter *ayn* equates to a glottal stop and sounds like a short 'ah!' sound from the back of the throat, as if one is being strangled! Foreigners often ignore it as being too strange to their ears but it is one of the most common letters and must be articulated if one wishes to speak Arabic correctly.

Because the *ayn* has no equivalent English letter it is transliterated as a small ^{c} above the line.

The *ghayn* is easier to say, equating to the French pronunciation of the 'r' in 'rue'. It is transliterated as *gh*.

Examples of the use of these letters are:

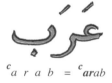

$^c a \ r \ a \ b \ = \ ^c arab$

This is the collective word in Arabic for 'Arabs'. It is important to articulate the sound of the ayn. (A single Arab would be *^{c}arabee*).

$gh \ a \ r \ b \ = \ gharb$

This means 'west' in Arabic .

At this point it is sensible to introduce the letter *yaa'*, which, although it is the last letter of the alphabet, is not only a consonant but also makes the long 'i' vowel. It is a connecting letter.

At the beginning and in the middle of a word the *yaa'* is written in the same way as the *baa'* family with a small hook, except that it has a characteristic two dots below the line:

At the end of a word, connected to a preceding letter or following a non-connector, the complete form is written:

connected to a preceding letter

following a non-connector

When acting as a consonant, *yaa'* is pronounced as the 'y' in 'yet' (and transliterated as *y*):

y a d = yad

This means 'a hand' in Arabic.

The Long 'i' Vowel

Whenever the short vowel *kasra* is followed by a *yaa'*, its associated letter, the combination makes a long 'i' vowel.

The long 'i' vowel is pronounced as the 'ee' in 'cheese' and transliterated as *ee*.

t̠   a   b   ee   b   =   t̠abeeb

The combination of the *kasra* and the *yaa'* make a long 'i' vowel. Because *t̠aa'* is an 'emphatic' letter it affects the sound of the *fatha* and this word is accurately pronounced as *tobeeb.* This means 'a physician' in Arabic.

Other Functions

Additionally, whenever a *fatha* is followed by a *yaa'* with a *sukoon* it forms the diphthong *ay* pronounced as 'ay' in 'hay':

b   ay   t   =   bayt

This means 'a house' in Arabic.

The final function of the *yaa'* is explained later in the book. (see pages 52 and 53).

These two letters are similar in shape but the tail of the *qaaf* is deeper than the *faa'* and falls below the line of writing. Otherwise, the dots clearly distinguish between them.* They are both connecting letters.

At the beginning of a word only the circular part at the front of each of the letters is written:

In the middle of a word, connected to a preceding and a following letter, the same:

But at the end of a word the full shape is shown:

The *faa'* is pronounced as the 'f' in 'foot' and transliterated as *f*. The *qaaf* is pronounced like the 'c' in 'caught' spoken from the very back of the throat‡ and transliterated as *q*.

* In Tunisia, Algeria and Morocco *faa'* is seen with the dot below the letter and *qaaf* with a single dot above it.

‡ A peculiarity of the *qaaf* is that sometimes it is pronounced as a 'g' in informal speech, and in Egypt, Lebanon and Syria it is articulated as a glottal stop!

ف
ق

Examples

s a f ee r = sa**feer**

The combination of the *kasra* and the *yaa* make a long 'i' vowel. This means 'an ambassador' in Arabic.

s
oo
q
=

sooq

The combination of the *damma* and the *waaw* make a long 'u' vowel. This means 'a market' in Arabic.

q i f = *qif!*

This a common road sign in Arab countries and means 'Stop!'

The *kaaf*, illustrated above in stand-alone form, resembles an English 'l' written backwards but with a little 's' in the bend, which is an integral part of the letter. It is a connecting letter.

The *kaaf* is unusual in that it changes shape completely at the beginning and in the middle of a word.

At the beginning of a word, connected to a following letter, it is shaped as below and the little 's' is dropped:

Similarly, in the middle of a word, connected to a preceding and a following letter it is the same shape without the 's':

But at the end of a word, connected to a preceding letter it appears as illustrated below:

The *kaaf* is pronounced as the 'k' in 'book' and is transliterated as *k*.

*k i t aa b = ki**taab***

The *fatha* and the *'alif* combine to make a long 'a' vowel. This means 'a book' in Arabic.

^ca s k a r ee = ^caskaree

The final *kasra* and the *yaa'* combine to make a long 'i' vowel. This means 'a soldier' or 'military' in Arabic.

*sh a r ee k = sha**reek***

The *kasra* and the *yaa'* combine to make a long 'i' vowel. This means 'a partner' in Arabic.

The shape of the *laam* in stand-alone and final form is similar to the *kaaf* but the *laam* goes below the line and there is no little 's' in the bend. *laam* is a connecting letter.

At the beginning of a word, connected to a following letter, only the vertical part is written:

In the middle of a word, connected to a preceding and a following letter, *laam* is written:

The *laam* cannot be confused with the *'alif* which is never joined to a following letter. At the end of a word *lamm* is written:

laam is pronounced as a light version of the 'l' as in 'lift'. It is transliterated as *l*.

The *laam* has a special shape when followed by an *'alif*. The two are then written in a combined form:

◆ Connected to a preceding letter:

◆ Not connected to a preceding letter: ﻻ

*th   aa   l   i   th = **thaalith***

The *fatha* and *'alif* make a long 'a' vowel. This is the adjective 'third' in Arabic.

Again, there can be no confusion between the *'alif* and the *laam* – in this word the first vertical stroke is not connected to the following letter and therefore is an *'alif* but the second vertical stroke is connected and therefore must be a *laam*.

*r   a   j   u   l = **rajul***

This means 'a man' in Arabic.

The *meem*, illustrated above in its stand-alone form, is pronounced as the 'm' in 'me' and transliterated as *m*. It is a connecting letter.

The principal characteristic of the *meem* is the small bead head written on the line of writing. At the beginning of a word, connected to a following letter, only this bead is shown:

In the middle of a word, connected to a preceding and a following letter, the same is true:

But at the end of a word connected to a preceding letter it is written in its full form:

The meem has a special form when one *meem* follows another and when a *meem* follows a *laam* but is always recognisable by the bead:

(See example on page 44.)

m a t̲ aa r = **ma*t̲*aar**

The combination of the *fatha* and the *'alif* make a long 'a' vowel. This means 'an airport' and is a common road sign in Arab countries.

j a m a l = **jam*a*l**

This word is pronounced ***gamal*** in Egypt and some other countries (see page 16). It is the Arabic for 'a camel'.

m a t̲ ᶜ a m = **ma*t̲* ᶜam**

This is the Arabic for 'a restaurant'. Note the stress is on the first syllable, the *t̲* is a deep, emphatic sound and the *ayn* should be clearly articulated (see page 32).

The *noon*, illustrated above in its stand-alone form, is basically a cup shape with a dot in the middle. The dot is an integral part of the letter and its principal recognition feature.

noon is a connecting letter. It is pronounced as the 'n' in English and transliterated as *n*.

At the beginning of a word, like the *baa'* family and the *yaa'*, it is written as a small hook but with the dot above it:

Similarly, in the middle of a word, connected to a preceding and a following letter, it is written:

But at the end of a word, the full form is written:

The exact shape of the *noon* may vary slightly to accommodate a letter connected to it but is always recognisable by the dot above the hook.

Examples

n   oo   r = noor

The *damma* followed by the *waaw* makes a long
'u' vowel. The *waaw* is a non-connector and therefore the *raa'* is written in stand-alone form.

This is one of the words meaning 'light' or 'a
light' in Arabic.

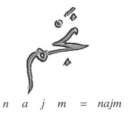

n   a   j   m   =   najm

This is the Arabic word for 'a star' (both literal
and metaphorical).

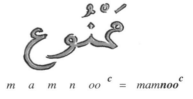

*m   a   m   n   oo   c = mam**noo**c*

The combination of the *damma* and the *waaw*
make a long 'u' vowel.

This means 'forbidden' in Arabic and appears in
numerous notices, such as 'no entry' and 'no
smoking'. (*See* page 116.)

The *haa'*, illustrated above in its stand-alone form, is a connecting letter. It is one of the more unusual, in that there is little resemblance between its various forms.

At the beginning of a word, connected to a following letter, it is similar to the stand-alone form:

But in the middle of a word, connected to a preceding and a following letter, its shape changes completely to one of these two alternatives:

either   or

The left hand version is most commonly found in print and the right hand one in handwriting.

Finally, at the end of a word, connected to a preceding letter, it is written:

The *haa'* is the second of the 'h' sounds in the Arabic alphabet, the first being the emphatic letter *ḥaa'* described on page 17.

The *haa'* sounds softer by comparison, like the normal English 'h' in 'he'. In Arabic it is articulated wherever it appears, even at the end of a word. The *haa'* is transliterated as *h* (as opposed to <u>h</u>).

It should also be noted that the shape of the final *haa'* is used for one of the 'supplement-ary' letters in Arabic but this is explained in the next chapter.

h   u   w   a   = **huwa**

The *fatha* over the *waaw* means that it is a consonant rather than a long 'u' vowel. This word is the third person singular of the personal pronouns – 'he'.

n   a   h   r   = *nahr*

This means 'a river' in Arabic.

w   a   j   ee   h   = **wajeeh**

This means 'a dignitary' in Arabic.

Table of the complete Arabic Alphabet
showing the letters in
all their forms

The Arabic Alphabet

The letters in all their forms in alphabetic order

Name of letter		Standing alone	a preceding letter	Connected to: a preceding & following letter	a following letter
أَلِف	'alif	ا	ﺎ	—	—
بَاء	baa'	ب	ﺐ	ﺒ	ﺑ
تَاء	taa'	ت	ﺖ	ﺘ	ﺗ
ثَاء	thaa'	ث	ﺚ	ﺜ	ﺛ
جِيم	jeem	ج	ﺞ	ﺠ	ﺟ
حَاء	_haa'_	ح	ﺢ	ﺤ	ﺣ
خَاء	khaa'	خ	ﺦ	ﺨ	ﺧ
دَال	daal	د	ﺪ	—	—
ذَال	dhaal	ذ	ﺬ	—	—
رَاء	raa'	ر	ﺮ	—	—
زَاء	zaa'	ز	ﺰ	—	—
سِين	seen	س	ﺲ	ﺴ	ﺳ
شِين	sheen	ش	ﺶ	ﺸ	ﺷ

Name of letter	Standing alone	Connected to: a preceding letter	a preceding & following letter	a following letter
صَاد saad	ص	ص	ـصـ	صـ
ضَاد daad	ض	ض	ـضـ	ضـ
طَاء taa'	ط	ط	ـطـ	ط
ظَاء dhaa'	ظ	ظ	ـظـ	ظ
عَيْن ᶜayn	ع	ع	ـعـ	عـ
غَيْن ghayn	غ	غ	ـغـ	غـ
فَاء faa'	ف	ف	ـفـ	فـ
قَاف qaaf	ق	ق	ـقـ	قـ
كَاف kaaf	ك	ك	ـكـ	كـ
لاَم laam	ل	ل	ـلـ	لـ
مِيم meem	م	م	ـمـ	مـ
نُون noon	ن	ن	ـنـ	نـ
هَاء haa'	ه	ـه	ـهـ	هـ
وَاو waaw	و	ـو	—	—
يَاء yaa'	ي	ي	ـيـ	يـ
هَمْزَة hamza	ء	(See following Chapter 4)		

4 Supplementary Letters

There are a number of supplementary letters and signs in Arabic and marks which affect pronunciation. These are explained below together with a note on Arabic punctuation.

Perhaps the most important special sign is the *hamza*. Although its main function is to act as a consonant, it is not, purely for historical reasons, usually regarded as a letter of the alphabet.

There are two kinds of *hamza*:

◆ The 'cutting' *hamza (hamzat-al-qaṭᶜ)* ﺀ

◆ The 'joining' *hamza (hamzat-al-waṣl)* ٱ

The cutting *hamza* acts in every way as a consonant, taking the short vowels or a *sukoon* but it never changes shape or connects to any other letter.

51

The cutting *hamza* is pronounced as a glottal stop which equates to the short catch in speech when, for example, a Cockney pronounces the word 'bitter' as 'bi'er'. This sound is often hard for a foreigner to discern, but it must be articulated to speak Arabic correctly.

The *hamza* is transliterated as an apostrophe '.

At the start of a word, the cutting *hamza* with its short vowel is always written over, or in the case of the *kasra* under, an *'alif*:

In all these cases the *'alif* acts only as a bearer or seat for the *hamza* and has no sound of its own. (This is the second major function of the *'alif* mentioned on page 10.)

The cutting *hamza* at the start of a word is not always shown in printed texts - simply the *'alif* on its own.

The cutting *hamza* also appears in the middle and end of words and can then be seated on an *'alif,* a *waaw* or a *yaa'* – again acting only as bearers with no sound of their own or it can be written independently. Unlike the initial *hamza*, the *hamza* in the middle or end of a word is always shown. When the *hamza* is seated on a *yaa'* the two dots are always omitted.

Examples

' *a n t a* = *'anta*

This word is the second person (masculine singular) personal pronoun 'you'.

r a ' s = *ra's*

This is the Arabic for 'a head' or 'a headland'.

s u ' aa l = *su'aal*

The *waaw* is only the bearer for the *hamza* and has no sound of its own. This means 'a question' in Arabic.

q aa ' i d = **qaa**'id

In this case the *hamza* is seated on a *yaa'* seat, without the dots. This is the Arabic for 'a leader', 'a commander' or 'a general'.

Some of the names of letters of the alphabet end in a final *hamza* without a seat and in this case it is printed slightly larger than normal:

baa'   ثاء *taa'*   فاء *faa'*

There are rules for determining the correct seat for the cutting *hamza* but these are complicated and certainly need not concern the beginner. However, for completeness, a résumé is given below.

At the beginning of a word the seat for the cutting *hamza* is always an *'alif*.

In the middle of a word the *hamza* sits on the letter associated with the preceding short vowel or the short vowel on the *hamza* itself. If these clash then priority is given in the order *kasra, damma, fatha*. If the *hamza* is preceded or followed by a long 'i' vowel then it sits on a *yaa'*. The dots of the *yaa'* are always omitted. Where the *hamza* carries a *fatha* and is preceded by a *waaw* or an *'alif* there is usually no seat.

At the end of a word the *hamza* is again written on the letter associated with the preceding short vowel but if there is no short vowel or a long vowel precedes the *hamza* then there is no seat.

hamzat-al-wasl

The definite article 'the' in Arabic is:  'al

and is attached to the word it qualifies. When a word with the definite article stands alone or is the first word in a sentence the *hamza* is a cutting *hamza* although it is not, by special custom, actually written, only the *fatha* short vowel over the *'alif:*

$$\text{ٱلْبَيْت}$$

'a l - b a y t 'al-bayt (the house)

However, when a word with the definite article follows another, the cutting *hamza* is replaced by the other kind of *hamza* – the joining *hamza* or *hamzat-al-wasl,* which looks like this: ‿

The joining *hamza* has no sound of its own but elides the first syllable of the word with the last short vowel of the preceding word. If there is no last short vowel then one is provided, usually a *kasra*.

If, for example the word above followed another, it would be written:

kh a r a j a   m i n   i ' l - b a y t   = **kha**raja min i'l-bayt

This means 'he went out from the house'

* The definite article is further explained on pages 85 and 95.

The joining *hamza* is only found at the start of a word seated on an *'alif*, mainly with the definite article but is not normally shown in unvowelled printed text.

The final vowelling of verbs such as **khara**ja above is dealt with in Chapter 8, Basic Grammar (see pages 91 and 92).

When two *'alifs* follow each other in the same word only one is written with the sign ‿ *madda* placed over it:

a   a   b   =   aab

The *'alif madda* is pronounced as a long *aa*. This word means August.

Exceptionally, in a few common words the long 'a' vowel is written as a short downstroke over the letter it follows and is known as a dagger *'alif*:

*h   aa   dh   aa   =   **haadhaa***

This word means 'this' in Arabic.

One word with dagger *'alif* which has an
unusual spelling is:

a   l   ll   aa   h = **'all**laah*

This is the Arabic word for God.

At the end of some words *'alif* appears:

This is called *'alif maqsoora* or shortened *'alif*.
It is pronounced as a short 'a' and transliterated
as *a*. (See examples on pages 102 and 109.)

This supplementary letter is only found at the end
of words. It is not considered part of the alphabet
because its function is primarily grammatical.

The *taa' marboota* uses the shape of the final
haa' combined with the two dots of the *taa'*
above it and is always preceded by a fatha:

standing alone   connected to a preceding letter

* By convention the *hamzat-al-qat* is not written on the *'alif* of
*'all**laah* and the dagger *'alif* is often replaced with a *fatha*.

A *taa' marboota* at the end of a word almost always indicates that it is feminine. (Arabic, like French has only two genders, masculine and feminine.)

taa' marboota means 'tied' *taa'* in Arabic.

When a word ending with a *taa' marboota* is on its own, only the preceding *fatha* is pronounced, *i.e.* the end of the word is pronounced as a short 'a' sound and transliterated as the short vowel *a*.

z   a w   j   a   = *zawja*

This word means 'a wife' in Arabic.

However, if anything is added to the word or it is followed by another word, then the *taa' marboota* is written and pronounced as a 't' (hence the description 'tied' *taa'*).

For example, if the suffix *ee*, meaning 'my' in Arabic, is added to the word above, then it is written and pronounced:

z   aw   j   a   t   ee = *zawjatee* (my wife)

The *taa' marboota* is further explained in Chapter 8 – Basic Grammar. (See pages 87 to 89.)

In fully vowelled Arabic text, such as the Holy Quran, classical literature and formal documents, it is customary to write the grammatical 'case endings' of words and pronounce them in recitations.

By 'case ending' is meant an ending indicating the grammatical role of a word in a sentence, whether it is the subject (nominative), the object (accusative) or the possessor (genitive).

These endings are indicated by using the short vowel signs and the process is called *tanween* or nunation.

tanween is only relevant to modern (unvowelled) text in one instance and for this reason in particular it is explained in simple terms below.

In fully vowelled text the case endings of 'definite' nouns and adjectives etc (*i.e.* 'the' as opposed to 'a' house), are indicated by short vowels written on the last letter of a word:

nominative	accusative	genitive

| *'al-baytu* | *'al-bayta* | *'al-bayti* |

The case endings of 'indefinite' nouns and adjectives (*i.e.* 'a' house) on the other hand, take the form of doubled short vowel signs written on the last letter of the word:

nominative	accusative	genitive

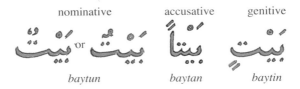

| *baytun* | *baytan* | *baytin* |

The only occasion when *tanween* is relevant in modern (unvowelled) text and everyday speech is with the accusative double *fatha* ending (an) which is used in a number of common words and particularly adverbs. It is often written with an additional *'alif* but this is not pronounced - only the 'an' of the *tanween*. This is the case with the words on the front cover of this book:

'ahlan wa sahlan - welcome

Other examples are:

*jid*dan – very

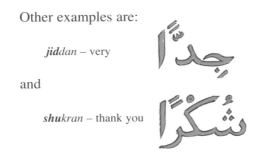

and

*shuk*ran – thank you

60

The double *fatha* (*an*) also appears over a *taa'*
marboota and in this case is pronounced *atan*:

ᶜaadatan – usually

In unvowelled text the sign of the double *fatha*
itself may not always be shown but the final *'alif*
or *taa' marboota* associated with it is always
written.

Finally, and only in vowelled text, the double
fatha ending will be seen written over a hamza
preceded by an *'alif* or followed by an *'alif*
maqsoora:

maa*'an*	**fa***tan*
normally pr. maa'	*normally pr. fata*
(water)	(young man)

Punctuation marks in Arabic are generally the
same as or mirror those in English:

Arabic ( ) « » \ ٪ ؟ ! : ؛ ، .

English ( ) " " / % ? ! : ; , .

Arabic Transcription

There is no standard method of transcribing foreign words in Arabic but the usual system outlined below may be helpful.

Both short and long vowels in foreign languages are often represented by the corresponding long vowel in Arabic. For example Hilton is usually transcribed in Arabic as *heeltoon*.

The letters p and v are either represented by *baa'* or *faa'* respectively or by the supplementary letters described below.

The following supplementary letters are sometimes used in Arabic:

Letter	Name	Used to represent English
پ	*pa*	p as in peel
ڤ	*vaf*	v as in victor
چ	*cheem*	ch as in chip*

These letters, and others, are in common use in certain non-Arabic speaking countries which use the Arabic script.

Finally, words in English where the letter 's' is followed by another consonant other than a 'w' are transcribed into Arabic as:

 *'iskutlandaa* (Scotland)

* In Egypt, where *jeem* is pronounced as a hard 'g', *cha* is often used to represent the sound 'j'.

Numbers

The figures below are those commonly used in all the Arab countries except Morocco, Algeria, Tunisia and Libya, where European figures are used:

1	١
2	٢
3	٣
4	٤
5	٥
6	٦
7	٧
8	٨
9	٩

Zero ◆

The Arabic zero should not be confused with a decimal point (normally a comma in Arabic) or the five with an English zero. Two and three in Arabic are very similar, as are seven and eight. Seven can best be remembered by picturing 'seVen'.

Surprisingly, compound numbers are written in the opposite direction to the Arabic script *i.e.* as in English, from left to right!

The numbers from 10 onwards are:

10	١٠
11	١١
12	١٢
13	١٣
14	١٤
15	١٥
16	١٦
17	١٧
18	١٨
19	١٩
20	٢٠
21	٢١

The year 2003 would be written:

The number 34.50 would be written:

$$٣٤٫٥٠$$

Fractions and percentages are written in the European style:

1/4   ¼   26 %   ٪٢٦

However, groups of compound numbers are organised in the same direction as the Arabic script and the date 24/09/35 would be written:

$$٣٥\٠٩\٢٤$$

The same is true of a combined compound number and letter. 6159 B could be written as:

ب٦١٥٩   or   ﻲﺑ:٦١٥٩

There are significant differences in the appearance of some of the figures in handwritten Arabic and this is explained in Chapter 7 – Handwriting.

The words for the numbers in grammatically correct Arabic are complicated by the fact that there are masculine and feminine forms and strict rules for their use. This is outside the scope of this book but is explained in any good Arabic grammar. There is, however, a colloquial or spoken form and these are listed in Chapter 9 – Useful Words and Phrases.

6
Calligraphy

It would be difficult to over-emphasise the importance of the art of calligraphy in the Islamic World, particularly of religious texts. Calligraphic inscription is everywhere in evidence in beautifully decorated architectural monuments, mosques, pottery, glass and metalwork and most of all in the countless handwritten copies of the Holy Quran itself.

Historically, the concept of alphabet was conceived in what was known as the Fertile Crescent – the region between Egypt and Mesopotamia, or present day Iraq – and the Arabic writing system is believed to have originated in the Aramaic script, the language of Jesus, and possibly the Nabataean and ancient Egyptian scripts as well.

However, when the Arabic script was first introduced into Makkah shortly before the revelation of the Holy Quran to the Prophet Muhammad, it was rudimentary and without vowels, dots or other diacritical marks. It was only with the coming of Islam that it began to develop into the form we know it today. This took place in several phases under the direction of the early Muslim Caliphs and was specifically motivated by the need accurately to preserve the word of God as enshrined in the Holy Quran.

The sacred nature of the language enshrined in the Holy Quran endowed the script with a special religious quality and it was for this reason, and because figurative art was restrained in Islam, that calligraphy became the foremost of the Islamic decorative arts and principally based on religious texts from the Holy Quran.

Modern Islamic art continues the calligraphic tradition in compositions based on extracts from the Holy Quran portrayed in a variety of designs including animals and birds.

Calligraphy is commonly used to decorate greetings cards sent on the occasion of the principal religious festivals:

As briefly mentioned in Chapter 2 the defining shape of the Arabic letters originated as a result of writing the script with the traditional reed pen or 'calamus'.

This was a short length of reed, or occasionally a fruit or rose wood stem, cut at an angle appropriate to the style of script:

Nib used for *nashkee, thulth* and *diwaanee* scripts

Nib used for Kufic and *ruq^c a* scripts

This explains why the letters, written with the reed at approximately 60° to the paper in a mainly clockwise direction, vary in thickness and why the dots are diamond shaped:

Writing the letter *baa'* with the traditional nib

Styles of Script

The phased development of the Arabic script resulted in the emergence of a great many different styles and designs. One of the earliest was the classic Kufic style, the first to become universally accepted throughout the Muslim empire:

An example of early Islamic Kufic script
Note the lack of dots, vowels and other diacritical marks

Among the many subsequently developed styles are:

naskh

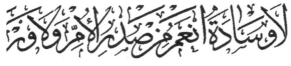

thulth

ruqᶜa

diwaanee

naskh is a common basis for printed scripts today, the ornamental *thulth* is generally used in mosque and manuscript decoration and
ruq^ca is the basis of handwriting throughout the Arab world.

Some of the modern printed fonts are illustrated below. They are very similar. A common newspaper and magazine font is Simplified Arabic:

١ ٢ ٣ ٤ ٥ ٦ ٧ ٨ ٩ تأكل من ثمر التفاح.
آه لأداء شذى نبات سهل الاسكا.

Simplified Arabic

١ ٢ ٣ ٤ ٥ ٦ ٧ ٨ ٩ تأكل من ثمر التفاح.
آه لأداء شذي نبات شهل الاسكا.

Mahdi

١ ٢ ٣ ٤ ٥ ٦ ٧ ٨ ٩ تأكل من ثمر التفاح.
آه لأداء شذي نبات شهل الاسكا.

Yasmin

١ ٢ ٣ ٤ ٥ ٦ ٧ ٨ ٩ تأكل من ثمر التفاح.
آه لأداء شذي نبات شهل الاسكا.

Fahdi

Modern institutions also employ calligraphy to produce attractive logos:

Logo of the airline Emirates

One can make out the letters of the word

'al-'imaaraat

The Arabic used in modern advertisements and notices can be particularly inventive. It is usually capable of analysis if one concentrates on the basic characteristics of the letters and uses a little imagination to decipher the Arabisation of the foreign words:

meetsoobeeshee (Mitsubishi)

baawaarfeen (Powerfin)

mooleeniks (Moulinex)

7 Handwriting

The purpose of this chapter is to assist the beginner to read handwritten script and to begin writing themselves.

Writing with a good hand requires application and practice, ideally with the help of a tutor but failing that by reference to the books mentioned in the bibliography.

In most of the Arab world handwriting is based on the *ruq{c}a* calligraphic style mentioned in the previous chapter:

حمل رجل مرة حزمة حطب سه الغابة

ruq{c}a

Handwriting modifies the ligatures and dots and alters the position of some of the letters in relation to one another. In addition, writing with a fountain pen or ball-point does not reproduce the variations in the thickness of the letters. That aside, handwritten script is remarkably similar to printed text.

The explanations that follow deal with each of the letters and numerals in turn and highlight the differences between the printed and handwritten versions. They also indicate the direction in which each letter is written.

The Letters

In stand-alone form, the *'alif* is written from the top and often slopes forward from the horizontal but in the middle or end of a word it is written from the bottom:

joined   standing alone

Printed   Handwritten

The top line of the *'alif madda* is often longer than the printed version:

Printed   Handwritten

baa' is written from right to left and more shallow at the start than the printed version. The dot is added afterwards:

Printed   Handwritten

The *taa'* and the *thaa'* are the same but the dots of the *taa'* and the *thaa'* are joined in handwriting:

Printed   Handwritten

Printed   Handwritten

At the start of a word these letters are often handwritten well above the line and unlike printing, the connection with the next letter slopes from top right to bottom left. This is a general feature of Arabic handwriting..

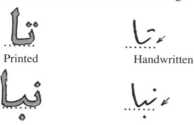

Printed · · · · · · · · Handwritten

Printed · · · · · · · · Handwritten

The *jeem*, the *ḥaa'* and the *khaa'* are written:

Printed · · · · · · · · Handwritten

The dots are added afterwards. A variety of ligatures is used when they are joined to other letters:

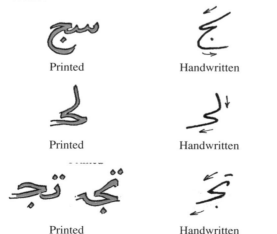

Printed · · · · · · · · Handwritten

Printed · · · · · · · · Handwritten

Printed · · · · · · · · Handwritten

The *daal* and *dhaal* are written:

Printed   Handwritten

the dot being added afterwards. The line from
a preceding letter joins from below the back of
the daal or dhaal which themselves stay above
the line of writing:

Printed   Handwritten

The *raa'* and the *zaa'* are written in the same
direction except that in this case the preceding
letter connects at the top of the raa' or zaa'
which themselves extend below the line:

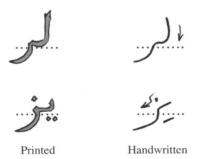

Printed   Handwritten

The seen is handwritten from right to left and
the hooks become a single line in handwriting:

Printed   Handwritten

The *sheen* is written in the same way and the dots of the *sheen*, written afterwards, are joined up as a little hat:

Printed   Handwritten

The *ṣaad* and the *ḍaad* are written:

Printed   Handwritten

When joined to a following letter remember to show the hook before the connection to the following letter:

Printed   Handwritten

The *ṭaa'* and the *ḍhaa'* are similar in shape but in this case the connecting line to the next letter has no hook. The vertical down-stroke and dots are added afterwards:

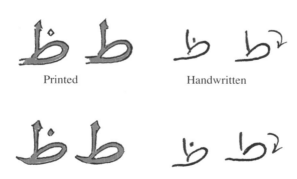

Printed   Handwritten

Printed   Handwritten

The *ayn* and the *ghayn* are written:

Printed   Handwritten

Printed   Handwritten

They have similarities with the *jeem* group at the end of a word but the loop at the top of the *ayn* and the *ghayn* is always closed:

Printed   Handwritten

The *faa'* and the *qaaf* are illustrated below. The dots of the *qaaf* are joined in handwriting:

Printed   Handwritten

Printed   Handwritten

kaaf is written:

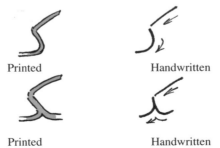

Printed   Handwritten

Printed   Handwritten

At the end of a word the little 's' of the *kaaf* is made a continuation of the final curve in hadwriting and virtually disappears:

Printed   Handwritten

kaaf is modified in handwriting when followed by *'alif* or *laam*:

Printed   Handwritten

laam, laam 'alif and *kaaf, laam, 'alif* are written:

Printed   Handwritten

meem, at the beginning of a word, can be written clockwise or anti-clockwise:

Printed   Handwritten

and in the middle and end of a word:

Printed   Handwritten

In various combinations, *meem* is written:

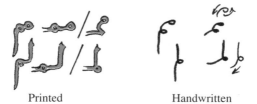

Printed   Handwritten

noon at the beginning and middle of a word is written:

Printed   Handwritten

But at the end of a word the dot is sometimes omitted or a completely different form used:

Printed   Handwritten

haa' at the beginning of a word is similar to the printed letter:

Printed   Handwritten

but in the middle of a word usually:

Printed   Handwritten

haa' at the end of a word connected to a preceding letter:

Printed   Handwritten

and after a non-connecting letter:

Printed   Handwritten

The *taa' marboota* is written as for the final *haa'* with the same variations but the two dots are either joined in a line or omitted:

Printed   Handwritten

The *waaw* is written:

Printed   Handwritten

The *yaa'* is written with the two dots connected:

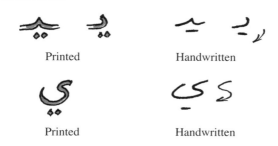

Printed   Handwritten

Printed   Handwritten

The *hamza* corresponds to the printed version
as does *'alif maqsoora*, *dagger 'alif* and other
marks where shown:

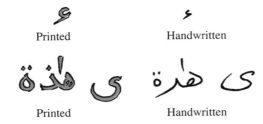

Printed   Handwritten

Printed   Handwritten

The following is typical of handwritten
script:

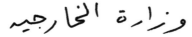

Handwritten script

وزارة الخارجية

Printed script

wizaarat al-khaarijiyya (Ministry of Foreign Affairs)

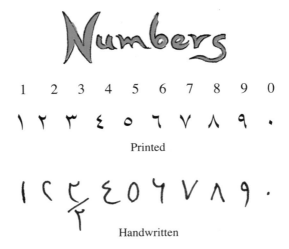

1	2	3	4	5	6	7	8	9	0
١	٢	٣	٤	٥	٦	٧	٨	٩	٠

Printed

Handwritten

8

Basic Grammar

Although Arabic as a Semitic language is structurally different from English, it is in some ways simpler to learn and the grammar more logical.

In common with all Semitic languages, a major feature of Arabic is that most words are based on a three-consonant root which is usually a verb.

For example, the three consonants *k* plus *t* plus *b* are the root in Arabic concerned with 'writing' and by putting vowels and other consonants around this root in various combinations, all the words to do with 'writing' are made:

kataba	to write he wrote
kaataba	to write to someone
kit**aab**	a book
kaatib	a clerk
maktab	an office
maktaba	a library/bookshop
mu**kaatib**	a correspondent/reporter
mak**toob**	written/a letter

Although not all words in Arabic conform to a set pattern, this feature certainly helps in an understanding of the structure of the language and its vocabulary.

There is no infinitive in Arabic (*e.g.* meaning 'to write') and so the third person singular of the verb (*i.e.* **kat**aba 'he wrote'), is used to describe the root, since this is the basic stem without prefix or suffix.

An Arabic dictionary lists words in alphabetical root order and then gives the derivatives, verbal and other. For example the word **mak**taba (a library) would be first looked up under the root *k t b* and then, within the *k t b* section, under '*m*' *k t b*.

Of the countless examples of three-consonantal roots are:

s l m –   the root concerned with 'peace' from which derive:
    silm and *salaam*   peace
    'islaam   submission
    muslim   Muslim

d r s –   the root concerned with 'learning' or 'study':
    darasa   to study
    darrasa   to teach
    dars   a lesson
    *mad***rasa**   a school

A good many of the derived meanings are not immediately obvious and there are also a number of four-consonantal roots but the three-consonant root is nevertheless the basis of most words.

The Definite Article

There is no indefinite article 'a' in Arabic and:

وَلَد *walad* – means 'a boy'

As mentioned on page 55, the definite article 'the' in Arabic is:

أَلْ

which is always attached to the word it qualifies and it is transliterated with a hyphen:

اَلْوَلَد *al-walad* – the boy

However, the cutting hamza on the first word in a sentence (or a word on its own) is normally omitted, even in vowelled text.

Sun Letters

The pronunciation of the definite article is affected by the letter following it. Fourteen of the letters of the Arabic alphabet are categorised as 'sun' letters and when the definite article is followed by a 'sun' letter the '*l*' of the article is not pronounced but assimilated by the 'sun' letter which is itself then doubled.

For example, the Arabic for 'a company' is:

شَرِكَة *sharika*

but *sheen* is a 'sun' letter and therefore the word for 'the company' would be written:

اَلشَّرِكَة and pronounced *ash-sharika*.

laam is also a 'sun' letter and when a word begins with a *laam* then the two *laams* are always written together:

اَللُّبْنَانِي

'al-ll**ubnaanee** – the Lebanese

The fourteen 'sun' letters are:

ت ث د ذ ر ز س

ش ص ض ط ظ ل ن

All other letters (known as 'moon' letters) are pronounced in the normal way:

اَلْبَيْت

'al-**bayt** – the house

Again, as mentioned on page 55, if a word with the definite article is not the first word in a sentence, the 'cutting *hamza*' is replaced by a 'joining *hamza*'.

Word Order

Word order in spoken Arabic is the same as in English - subject, verb and object. However, in formal written Arabic the verb is usually put first, then followed by the subject and the object. For example in spoken Arabic:

اَلْوَلَد كَتَبَ ٱلْكِتَاب

'al-**walad kat**ab '*l*-kit**aab** – The boy wrote the book

But in written Arabic:

كَتَبَ ٱلْوَلَدُ ٱلْكِتَاب

kataba '*l*-**walad** '*l*-kit**aab** – Wrote the boy the book

Gender

As explained on page 58, nouns in Arabic are either masculine or feminine. Nouns referring only to females may be assumed to be feminine as may most nouns ending in *taa' marboota*.

The remainder are mostly masculine but there are exceptions which have to be learnt.

Plurals

There is a special way of saying 'two' of anything in Arabic and this is called the 'dual'. The 'dual' is formed by adding *aan* or *ayn* to a noun, depending on the case, but in speech it is always *ayn*:

وَلَدَين   *wala**dayn*** – two boys

If the noun ends in *taa' marboota* then the ending is written *atayn*:

شَرِكَتَين   *sharika**tayn*** – two companies

From three onwards plurals are formed in two ways, described as 'sound' or 'broken'.

'Sound' plurals of masculine nouns referring to people, form their plural by adding either *een* or *oon* depending on the 'case' but in speech it is always *een*:

مُسْلِم   ***mus**lim*   Muslim

مُسْلِمين   *muslim**een***   Muslims

'Sound' plurals of feminine words ending in *taa'
maboota* are formed by adding *aat*:

شَرِكَة   **shari**ka – a company

شَرِكَات   **shari**kaat – companies

Other plurals are of the 'broken' type. In this
case the root of a word remains the same but
the vowels are changed. There are a number of
patterns of 'broken' plural although it is not
possible to tell which is used for any particular
noun and the plural of each word has to be
learnt. Examples of typical 'broken' plurals are:

وَلَد	*walad*	–	a boy
أَوْلَاد	*'awlaad*	–	boys
بَيْت	*bayt*	–	a house
بُيُوت	*buyoot*	–	houses
شَيْء	*shai'*	–	a thing
أَشْيَاء	*'ashyaa'*	–	things
مَدْرَسَة	*madrasa*	–	a school
مَدَارِس	*madaaris*	–	schools
بَاب	*baab*	–	a door
أَبْوَاب	*'abwaab*	–	doors

88

In spoken Arabic, when words, as opposed to figures, are used to qualify a noun between 'three' and 'ten', the noun is put in the plural as in English:

ثَلاَثَة أَوْلاَد

thalaatha 'awlaad
three boys

However, surprisingly, from eleven onwards the noun is put in the singular:

عِشْرِين وَلَد

ʿishreen walad
twenty boys

In written Arabic the rules governing the agreement of written numbers with their nouns is more complicated and even some Arabs choose to avoid their use by using figures instead.

Adjectives must agree with their noun and if a noun has the definite article then so must the adjective:

اَلْوَلَد ٱلصَّغِير

'al-walad 'as-sagheer
the small boy

The adjective must also agree with the noun in gender:

بَيت كَبِير

bayt kabeer
a big house

but شَرِكَة صَغِيرَة

sharika sagheera*
a small company

---

* *taa' marboota* is added to the adjective to make it feminine.

Where an adjective qualifies people, it takes a sound plural:

أَوْلاد كَثيرين   *'awlaad katheereen*
many boys

بَنَات كَثيرات   *banaat katheeraat**
many girls

But when describing plural objects or animals then the adjective is put in the feminine singular by adding a *taa' marboota:*

شَرِكَات كَبيرَة   *sharakaat kabeera**
big companies

The comparative of most adjectives takes the following form:

كَبير   *kabeer* – big/great

أَكْبَر   *'akbar* – bigger/greater

رَخيص   *rakhees* – cheap

أَرْخَص   *'arkhas* – cheaper

كَثير   *katheer* – many

أَكْثَر   *'akthar* – more

and   الأَكْبَر   *'al-akbar* – the biggest or greatest

* The plural of the *taa' marboota* ة is ات pronounced *aat*. This is also the feminine sound plural ending.

Verbs

As mentioned on pages 83 and 84, a major feature of the Arabic language is that most words are based on a three-consonant root, usually a verb.

The derivatives of each verbal root include other verbs which are formed from the root on fixed patterns. For example **kaa***taba*, with an *'alif* placed after the *k* is the Arabic verb meaning 'to correspond with'. There is provision for up to ten forms of any verb, although this subject is outside the scope of this book.

Arabic verbs have only two tenses, one for the past and another for both the present/future. For example:

كَتَبَ **katab(a)*** means 'he wrote'

يَكْتُبُ **yaktub** means 'he is writing' or 'he will write'

However, in order to leave no doubt when the future tense is intended, the participle *sawf* or the prefix *sa* are used:

e.g. he will write سَوْفَ يَكْتُبُ *sawf **yaktub***

or

سَيَكْتُبُ *sa**yaktub***

One peculiarity of Arabic is that there is no verb 'to be' in the present tense. It does not exist, and:

اَلْوَلَد صَغِير *'al-**walad** ṣagheer*
means 'the boy (is) small'

The past and future tenses of the verb 'to be' are dealt with later in the chapter.

* The final short vowel is omitted in informal speech.

Simple regular verbs in the past tense such as
katab(a) 'he wrote' are formed by attaching
suffixes to the root:

كَتَبْتُ **katabt**(u)* I wrote

كَتَبْتَ **katabt**(a)* you(masc)wrote

كَتَبْتِ **katabt**(i)* you (fem) wrote

كَتَبَ **katab**(a)* he wrote

كَتَبَتْ **katab**at she wrote

كَتَبْنَا **katab**naa we wrote

كَتَبْتُم **katabtum** you (pl) wrote

كَتَبُوا **katab**oo they wrote

There is no need to use the subject pronoun 'I'
'you', 'he', 'she', etc in Arabic since:

كَتَبَ **katab**(a)* means 'he wrote'

The combined present/future tense is formed by
adding prefixes and sometimes a suffix, to the root:

اَكْتُبُ **'aktub**(u)* I write/will write

تَكْتُبُ **taktub**(u)* you (masc) write/will write

تَكْتُبِين **taktub**ee(n)* you (fem) write/will write

يَكْتُبُ **yaktub**(u)* he writes/will write

تَكْتُبُ **taktub**(u)* she writes/will write

نَكْتُبُ **naktub**(u)* we write/will write

تَكْتُبُونَ **taktub**oo(na)* you (pl) write/will write

يَكْتُبُونَ **yaktub**oo(na)* they write/will write

This is the pattern for most regular verbs.
However, the change of the second short vowel
(from *a* to *u* in this case) varies and must be
learnt for each verb.

* The letters and vowels in brackets are normally omitted in
informal speech.

Verb 'to be' / The Negative

The past tense is of a different pattern:

كُنْتُ	*kunt(u)**	I was
كُنْتَ	*kunt(a)**	you(masc)were
كُنْت	*kunt(i)**	you (fem) were
كَانَ	*kaan(a)**	he was
كَانَتْ	**kaan**at	she was
كُنَّا	**kunn**aa	we were
كُنْتُم	**kun**tum	you (masc pl) were
كَانُو	**kaan**oo	they (masc pl) were

The combined present and future tense is:

أَكُونُ	'*akoon(u)** *	I will be
تَكُونُ	*takoon(u)**	you (masc) will be
تَكُونِين	*takoonee(n)**	you (fem) will be
يَكُونُ	*yakoon(u)**	he will be
تَكُونُ	*takoon(u)**	she will be
نَكُونُ	*nakoon(u)**	we will be
تَكُونَ	*takoonoo(na)**	you (pl) will be
يَكُونُونَ	*yakoonoo(na)**	they (masc pl) will be

Among several ways of expressing the negative of a verb are placing particles in front of it:

In the past tense مَا *maa*

مَا كَتَبَ   *maa **katab**(a)* – He did not write

In the present and future tenses لا *laa*

لا يَكْتُب   *laa **yaktub*** – He does not/will not write

---

* The letters and vowels in brackets are normally omitted in informal speech.

93

Personal Pronouns

أَنَا	*'an*aa	I
أَنْتَ	*'an*ta	you (masc sing)
أَنْتِ	*'an*ti	you (fem sing)
هُوَ	*hu*wa	he/it
هِيَ	*hi*ya	she/it
نَحْنُ	*nah*nu	we
أَنْتُمْ	*'an*tum	you (masc pl)
هُمْ	*hum*	they

Possession

This is expressed by adding suffixes to a noun:

ـِي	*ee*	my
ـَكَ	*ak(a)**	yours (masc sing)
ـِك	*ik(i)**	yours fem
ـهُ	*uh(u)**	his
ـهَا	*haa*	hers
ـنَا	*naa*	ours
ـكُمْ	*kum*	yours (masc pl)
ـهُمْ	*hum*	theirs (masc pl)

* In informal speech the short vowels in brackets are not pronounced.

For example:

بَيْتِي   *bayt + ee = baytee* and
means 'my house'

If a suffix is added to a *taa' marboota* it
becomes a *taa'* (see page 58):

شَرِكَتِي   *sharika + ee = **shar**ikatee*
meaning 'my company'.

The same suffixes are used as objects of a verb
except that ي *ee* becomes نِي *nee*:

ضَرَبَنِي   *darab + nee = darabnee*
and means 'he struck me'.

The Construct State

There is a special way of expressing possession
between two nouns in Arabic known as 'the
Construct State'. It directly equates to the
English way of saying 'the boy's house'. In
Arabic the words are reversed - the word 'house'
being followed by 'the boy':

بَيْت ٱلْوَلَد   *bayt 'al-walad*

In Arabic this means '(the) house (of) the boy'.
The definite article on the first word and the 'of'
before the second word are understood.

Proper names are always assumed to be definite and therefore 'Ahmed's house' *i.e.* 'the house of Ahmed', would be written:

بَيْت أَحْمَد   *bayt 'ahmed*

Questions

In spoken Arabic a question is often expressed by the tone of voice but in the written language one of the most common methods is to preface a sentence with the word *hal:*

هَلْ كَتَبْتَ ٱلْكتَاب؟

hal katabta 'l-kitaab?
Did you write the book?

One Letter Particles

The following one-letter participles and pre-positions are attached to a following word and have the meanings indicated:

وَ	*wa*	and
لـ	*li*	for *or* belong to
بـ	*bi*	by *or* with
فَ	*fa*	thus, therefore *or* so

وَكُلُّ عَامٍ وَأَنْتُمْ بِخَيرٍ

wa-kull ʿaamin wa-'antum bi-khayr
and every year and (I hope) you (are) with health
(part of the greeting printed on page 115)

When *laam* with *kasra* (لِ) is written before a
word with the definite article, the *'alif/hamza* of
the article is dropped and the remaining two
laams are connected:

لِلبَيْت

li-lbayt
for the house

One always needs to be aware of the possibility
that one of the above letters at the beginning of a
word is a particle and not an integral part of the
word.

There is of course much more to Arabic
grammar than this but it is hoped that this simple
introduction will encourage further study.

97

9
Useful Words and Phrases

This chapter contains a brief selection of useful words and phrases which might be encountered in the Arab world. They are set out under the following sections:

Administrative Terms
Arab Names
Cities
Countries
Geographical Terms
Ministries
Money, Weights and Measures
Numbers
Religious Terms
Signs and Notices
Titles and Ranks
Useful Phrases

Notes:

Short vowels are included as a guide, but would not normally be written in modern text.

The stress syllable is shown in bold type.

Unusual pronunciation is prefaced in transliteration by the abbreviation 'pr'.

Administrative Terms

branch	فَرْع	*far*^c
city	مَدينة	*ma**deen**a*
country	دَوْلَة	***daw**la*
district	قَضَاء	***qad**aa'*
or	مُقَاطَعَة	*mu**qaata**^ca*
region/district	إِقْلِيم	*'iq**leem***
department	دائِرَة	***daa**'ira*
ministry	وزَارَة	*wi**zaara***
municipality	بَلَدِيَّة	*bala**diyya***
office	مَكْتَب	***mak**tab*
tax (taxes)	ضَرِيبَة (ضَرَائِب)	*dareeba (daraa'ib)*
town	بَلَد	***bal**ad*
province	مُحَافَظة	*mu**haaf**adha*

Arab Names

The following is a selection of Arab male and female first names:

Abdulla	عَبْدُاللَّه	^c*ab**dull**ah**
Abdul-Rahman	عَبْدُ الرَّحْمَن	^c*abdu 'l-rah**man**

---

* The word ^c*abd* in a name, meaning literally 'servant of', is commonly linked to an attribute to God, in the first case 'servant of God', and secondly 'servant of the merciful'. Always refer to such a person by their full name and never refer to someone simply as 'Abdul'.

Adil	عَادِل	*caadil*
Ahmed/Ahmad	أَحْمَد	*'ahmad*
Ali	عَلِي	*calee*
Isa	عِيسَى	*ceesaa*
Faisal	فَيْصَل	*faysal*
Hamad	حَمَد	*hamad*
Hassan	حَسَن	*hasan*
Hussein	حُسَيْن	*husain*
Ibrahim	إِبْرَاهِيم	*'ibraheem*
Jabir	جَابِر	*jaabir*
Ja'far	جَعْفَر	*jacfar*
Jamil	جَمِيل	*jameel*
Khalid	خَالِد	*khaalid*
Khaleel	خَلِيل	*khaleel*
Kamaal	كَمَال	*kamaal*
Maajid	مَاجِد	*maajid*
Majeed	مَجِيد	*majeed*
Mahmood	مَحْمُود	*mahmood*
Mas'ood	مَسْعُود	*mascood*
Mohammed	مُحَمَّد	*muhammad*
Musa	مُوسَى	*moosa*
Mustafa	مُصطَفَى	*mustafa*
Nasser	نَاصِر	*naasir*
Omar	عُمَر	*cumar*
Saalah	صَالِح	*saalih*
Salim	سَالِم	*saalim*

Saleem	سَليم	*saleem*
Samir	سَمير	*sameer*
Sulaiman	سُلَيْمَان	*sulaymaan*
Sultan	سُلطَان	*sultaan*
Taariq	طَارق	*taariq*
Usama	أُسَامَة	*'usaamah*
Wajeeh	وَجيه	*wajeeh*
Yusif	يُوسُف	*yoosuf*

N.B. Sometimes a man may be referred to as *'abu* (أَبُو)
which means 'father of', followed by another name, often
that of his first born son, e.g. *'abu yoosuf*.

Female Names

Abeer	عَبِير	^c*abeer*
Aisha	عَائِشَة	^c*aa'isha*
Amal	آمَال	*aamaal*
Fareeda	فَرِيدَة	*fareeda*
Fatima	فَاطِمَة	*faatima*
Fauzia	فَوْزِيَّة	*fawziyya*
Hana	هَنَاء	*hanaa*
Hanan	حَنَان	*hanaan*
Huda	هُدَى	*huda*
Khadija	خَدِيجَة	*khadeeja*
Laila	لَيْلَى	*layla*

Marwa	مَرْوَة	*marwa*
Muna	مُنَى	*muna*
Nabeela	نَبِيلَة	*nabeela*
Najma	نَجْمَة	*najma*
Rania	رَانْيَا	*raanyaa*
Reem	رِيم	*reem*
Rula	رُولاَ	*roolaa*
Safa'a	صَفَاء	*safaa'*
Safia	صَفِيَّة	*safiyya*
Salwa	سَلْوَى	*salwa*
Shukran	شُكْرَان	*shukraan*
Taima'a	تَيْمَاء	*taymaa'*
Yasmin	يَاسَمِين	*yaasmeen*
Yumna	يُمْنَى	*yumnaa*
Zainab	زَيْنَب	*zaynab*

N.B. Sometimes a woman may be referred to as *'umm* (أُمّ)
which means 'mother of', followed by another name, often that
of her first born son or if no son, her first born daughter, e.g.
'umm kulthoom, a famous Egyptian singer.

Cities

Abu Dhabi	أَبُو ظَبِيّ	*'aboo dhabee*
Alexandria	اَلإِسْكَنْدَرِيَّة	*'al-'iskandariyya*
Algiers	اَلْجَزَائِر	*'al-jazaa'ir*
Amman	عَمَّان	*ᶜammaan*
Baghdad	بَغْدَاد	*baghdaad*

103

Beirut	بَيْرُوت	*bayroot*
Cairo	اَلْقَاهِرَة	*'al-qaahirah*
Casablanca	اَلدَّار اَلبَيْضَاء	*'al-daar 'l-baydaa'*
Damascus	دمَشْق	*dimashq*
Dhahran	اَلظَّهْرَان	*'adh-dhahraan*
Doha	اَلدُّوحَة	*'ad-dooha*
Dubai	دُبَي	*dubai*
Jeddah	جدَّة	*jidda*
Jerusalem	اَلْقُدْس	*'al-quds*
Khartoum	اَلْخَرْطُوم	*'al-khartoom*
Manama	اَلْمَنَامَة	*'al-manaama*
Makkah	مَكَّة اَلْمُكَرَّمَة	*makka 'l-mukarrama*
Muscat	مَسْقَط	*masqat*
Oman	عُمَان	*ᶜumaan*
Port Said	بُور سَيِّد	*boor saieed*
Rabat	اَلرَّبَاط	*'ar-rabaat*
Riyadh	اَلرِّيَاض	*'ar-reeaad*
Sana'a	صَنْعَاء	*sanᶜaa'*
Sharjah	اَلشَّارِقَة	*'ash-shaariqa*
		(but pr. *shaarja*)
Suez	اَلسُّوَيْس	*'as-sooways*
Tangier	طَنْجَة	*tanja*
Tripoli	طَرَابُلْس	*taraablus*
Tunis	تُونِس	*toonis*

Countries

Algeria	ٱلْجَزَائِر	'al-jazaa'ir
Bahrain	ٱلْبَحْرَين	'al-ba**hrayn**
Egypt	مِصْر	mi*sr*
Iraq	ٱلْعِرَاق	'al-*c*iraaq
Jordan	ٱلأُرْدُن	'al-l'**urdun**
Kuwait	ٱلْكُوَيْت	'al-koo**wait**
Lebanon	لُبْنَان	lub**naan**
Libya	لِيبْيَا	lee**beeyaa**
(The Kingdom of) Morocco	ٱلْمَمْلَكَةُ ٱلْمَغْرِبية	'al-**mamlaka** 'l-maghrib**iyya**
Oman	عُمَان	*c*u**maan**
Palestine	فلَسْطِين	filas**teen**
Qatar	قَطَر	qa*t*ar
(The Kingdom of) Saudi Arabia	ٱلْمَمْلَكَة ٱلْعَرَبَية ٱلسُّعُودِية	'al-mamlaka 'l-*c*arabiyya 's-sa*c*oodiyya
Sudan	ٱلسُّودَان	'as-soo**daan**
Syria	سُورِيَّة	soor**iyy**a
Tunisia	تُونِس	**toon**is
United Arab Emirates	ٱلإمَارَات ٱلْعَرَبَية ٱلْمُتَّحِدَة	'al-imaa**raat** 'l-*c*arab**iyya** 'l-mutta**h**ida
Yemen	ٱلْيَمَن	'al-**yam**an

Geographical Terms

Arabian Gulf	اَلْخَلِيج ٱلْعَرَبِي	'al-khaleej 'l-*arabee*
Middle East	اَلشَّرْق ٱلأَوْسَط	'ash-sharq 'l-*awsat*
Gulf of Oman	خَلِيج عُمَان	khaleej *umaan*
Mediterranean Sea	اَلْبَحْر ٱلأَبْيَض ٱلمُتَوَسِّط	'al-bahr 'l-'**abyad** 'l-muta**wassit**
Red Sea	اَلْبَحْر ٱلأَحْمَر	'al-bahr 'l-'ahmar
Rub Al Khali	اَلرُّبْع ٱلْخَالِي	'ar-rub* 'l-**kha**alee

Ministries

Ministry of:	وِزَارَة :	wi**zaa**rat:
Agriculture	ٱلزِّرَاعَة	'z-ziraa*a
Aviation	ٱلطَّيَرَان	't-tayraan
Commerce	ٱلتِّجَارَة	't-tijaara
Communications	ٱلمُوَاصَلَات	'l-muwaasilaat
Defence	ٱلدّفَاع	'd-difaa*
Development	ٱلإعْمَار /ٱلتَعْمِير /ٱلتَّطْوِير	'l-'i *maar/'t-ta*meer/ 't-tatweer
Economics	ٱلإقْتِصَاد	'l-iqtisaad
Education	ٱلتَّرْبِيَة /ٱلمعَارِف /ٱلتَعْلِيم	't-tarbeea/'l- ma*aarif/'t-ta*leem
Finance	ٱلمَالِيَّة	'l-maaliyya

Foreign Affairs	ٱلْخَارِجِيَّة	*'l-khaariji**yya***
Health	ٱلصِّحَّة	*'s-**sihh**a*
Industry	ٱلصِّنَاعَة	*'s-**sinaa**^ca*
Interior	ٱلدَاخِلِيَّة	*'d-daakhil**iyya***
Justice	ٱلْعَدْل/ٱلْعَدْلِيَّة	*'l-^c**adl**/'l-^c**adl**iyya*
Labour	ٱلْعَمَل	*'l-^c**am**al*
Marine (Navy)	ٱلْبَحْرِيَّة	*'l-ba**hri**yya*
National Economy	ٱلْإِقْتِصَاد ٱلْوَطَنِي	*'l-'iqti**saad** 'l-**wat**anee*
National Guidance	ٱلْإِرْشَاد اَلْوَطَنِي	*'l-'ir**shaad** 'l-**wat**anee*
Public Works	ٱلْأَشْغَال ٱلْعَامَّة	*'l-'ash**ghaal** 'l-^c**aam**ma*
Social Affairs	ٱلشُّؤُون ٱلْإِجْتِمَاعِيَّة	*'sh-shu'**oon**/'l-'ijtimaa^c**iyya***
Transport	ٱلنَّقْل	*'n-naql*

Money Weights and Measures

acre, feddan	فَدَّان	*fad**daan***
bank	مَصْرِف / بَنْك	*ma**sr**if/bank*
bureau de change	مَكْتَب ٱلصَّرَّاف	*mak**tab** 's-**sarraaf***

centimetre	سَنْتِمِتْر	**san**timitre
dinar	دينَار	**dee**naar
dirham	درْهَم	**dir**ham
dollar	دُولار	**doo**laar
euro	أُورُو	'**oo**roo
feddan, acre - *see* acre		
foot/feet	قَدَم / أَقدَام	**qad**am/**aq**daam
fils	فِلْس	*fils*
gallon	جَالُون	**gaa**loon
gramme	غْرَام	*ghraam*
hectare	هكْتَار	**hik**taar
inch	إنْش / بوُصَة	'*insh*/**boo**ṣa
kilogram	كيلُوغْرَام / كيلُو	**kee**looghraam/**kee**loo
kilometre	كيلُومِتْر	**kee**loomitr
lira	ليرَة	**lee**ra
litre	لِتْر	*litr*
metre	مِتْر	*mitr*
millimetre	ملِّيمِتْر	**mill**eemitr
mile	ميل	*meel*
piastre	قرْش / غِرْش	*qirsh*/*ghirsh*
pound, lira	ليرَة	**lee**ra
rial, riyal	ريَال	**ree**aal
sterling	إسْتِرْلينِي	'*istir***lee**nee
ton	طَنّ / طُنّ	ṯ*ann*/ṯ*unn*

Numbers

one	وَاحِد	**waa**hid
two	إِثْنَين	'ith**nayn**
three	ثَلاَثَة	tha**laa**tha
four	أَرْبَعَة	**'arba**^ca
five	خَمْسَة	**kham**sa
six	سِتَّة	sitta
seven	سَبْعَة	**sab**^ca
eight	ثَمَانِية	tha**maa**niyya
nine	تِسْعَة	**tis**^ca
ten	عَشَرَة	^c**ash**ara
twenty	عِشْرِين	^cish**reen**
fifty	خَمْسِين	kham**seen**
hundred	مِئَة	**mi**'a
thousand	أَلْف	'alf
million	مِلْيُون	mil**yoon**

Religious Terms

Allah	اَللَّه*	**'all**laah
Eid Al Adha	عِيد اَلأَضْحَى	^ceed 'l-**ad** haa
Eid Al Fitr	عِيد اَلفِطْر	^ceed 'l-**fi**tr

* By convention *'all*laah is written either with a *shadda* and a dagger *'alif* or a *shadda* and a *fatha*.

109

Islam	اَلْإِسْلاَم	'al-'islaam
God willing	إِنْ شَاءَ ٱللّٰه*	'in shaa' 'alllaah
Pilgrim	حَاجّ	_haajj_
Pilgrimage	حَجّ	_hajj_
Prophet	نَبِيّ	nabiyy (pr. nabee)
Thanks be to God	اَلْحَمْدُ لِلّٰه	'al-_hamdu lillaah_
The Holy Quran	اَلْقُرْآن اَلْكَرِيم /	'al-quraan 'l-
	اَلْقُرْآن اَلشَّرِيف	kareem/'al-qooraan
		'sh-shareef

Signs and Notices

Airport	مَطَار	ma**taar**
Ambulance	إِسْعَاف	'is^caaf
Arrivals	اَلْقَادِمُون	'al-qaadi**moon**
Bank	مَصْرِف / بَنْك	**ma**s**rif/bank**
Barber	حَلَّاق	hall**aaq**
Bookshop	مَكْتَبَة	**mak**taba
Bureau de change	مَكْتَب ٱلصَّرَّاف	**mak**tab 's-_sarr_**aaf**
Bus station	مَحَطَّة ٱلأَوْتُبِيس	maha**tt**at 'l-**awt**oobees
Café	مَقْهَى	**maq**ha
Centre (for)	مَرْكَز لِ ...	**mar**kaz (li...)
Closed (shop)	مُغْلَق	**mugh**laq

* By convention 'alllaah is written either with a *shadda* and a dagger 'alif or a *shadda* and a *fatha*. (*See* page 57.)

Company	شَرِكَة	**shar**ika
Consulate	قُنْصُلِيَّة	**quns**uliyya
Customs	جُمْرُك	**jum**ruk
Danger!	خَطَر!	**kha**tar!
Departures	اَلمُغَادِرُون	'al-mu**ghaad**iroon
Entrance	دُخول	du**khool**
Exhibition	مَعْرَض	**ma**ᶜradh
Exit	خُروج	khu**rooj**
Fire Extinguisher	مِطفَأَة حَرِيق	**mit**fa'a **har**eeq
Forbidden	مَمْنُوع	mam**noo**ᶜ
Hospital	مُسْتَشْفَى	mu**stashf**a
Hotel	فُنْدُق	**fun**duq
Lift	مِصعَد	**mis**ᶜad
Military Camp	ثَكْنَة/مُعَسْكَر	muᶜ**askar**/**thakn**a
Military Area	مِنطَقَة عَسْكَرِيَّة	mintaqa ᶜaskar**iyya**
Mortal Danger	خَطَر ٱلمَوْت	**kha**tar 'l-mawt
Museum	مَتْحَف	**mathaf**
No entry	مَمْنُوع ٱلدُخُول	mam**noo**ᶜ 'd-du**khool**
No parking	مَمْنُوع ٱلوُقُوف	mam**noo**ᶜ 'l-wu**qoof**
No photography	مَمْنُوع ٱلتَصوير	mam**noo**ᶜ 't-tas**weer**
No smoking	مَمْنُوع ٱلتَدْخِين	mam**noo**ᶜ 't-tadkheen
Open	مَفْتُوح	maf**tooh**
Palace	قَصْر	**qas**r
Passports	جَوَاز سَفَر	jaw**aaz saf**ar

Police	شُرْطَة	**shur**ta
Police Station	مَخْفَر ٱلشُّرْطَة	**makh**far 'sh-**shur**ta
Port	مِينَاء	**meen**aa'
Private	خَاصْ	khaas
pull	إسْحَب	'**is**hab
push	إدْفَع	'**idfa**ᶜ
Restaurant	مَطْعَم	**mat**ᶜam
School	مَدْرَسَة	mad**rasa**
Stop!	قِفْ!	qif!
Tailor	خَيَّاط	khai**yaat**
Taxi	تَكْسِي لِلإجْرَة	**tak**see lil-'ijra
	- sign on taxi for hire	
Telephone	تَلَفُون / هَاتِف	tala**foon**/**haa**tif
Toilet	دَوْرَة ٱلمِيَاه / حَمَّام	**dawra** 'l-meey**aah**/
		hum**maam**
Men	رِجَال	ri**jaal**
Women	سَيِّدَات	sayyi**daat**
University	جَامِعَة	**jaami**ᶜa

Titles and Ranks

agent	وَكِيل	wa**keel**
ambassador	سَفِير	sa**feer**
assistant	مُسَاعِد	musaa**ᶜid**
Brigadier	عَمِيد	ᶜa**meed**

Captain/Chairman/ Chief	رَئِيس	ra'ees
Chief of Staff	رَئِيس ٱلأَركَان	ra'ees 'l-'arkaan
clerk	كَاتِب	kaatib
Colonel	عَقِيد	ᶜaqeed
Commander	قَائِد	qaa'id
consul	قُنصُل	qunsul
dentist	طَبِّيب ٱلأَسنَان	tabbeeb 'l-'asnaan
deputy	نَائِب	naa'ib
director	مُدِير	mudeer
doctor	طَبِّيب	tabbeeb

Excellency.... (form of address)

- Governor, Ambassador or Director General	سَعَادَة	saᶜaada
- Minister	مَعَالِي	maᶜaalee
- President or Prime Minister	فَخَامَة	fakhaama
- Prime Minister	دَولَة	dawla
Governor	مُحَافِظ	muhaafidh
Highness	سُمُوّ	sumoo
His Royal Highness	صَاحِب ٱلسُّمُوّ	saahib 's-sumoo
Judge	حَاكِم	haakim
Lieutenant	مُلَازِم أَوَل	mulaazim 'awwal
Lieutenant Colonel	مُقَدَّم	muqaddam

Major	رَائِد	**ra**'id
Major-General	لِواء	liw**aa**'
manager/director	مُدِير	mu**deer**
mayor	رَئِيس ٱلبَلَدِيَّة	ra'**ees** 'l-bala**diyya**
minister	وَزِير	wa**zeer**
Mr.	سَيِّد	**say**yid
officer	ضَابِط	**daa**bi_t_
President	رَئِيس	ra'**ees** 'l-
(of the Republic)	ٱلجُمْهُورِيَّة	jumhoo**riyya**
Prime Minister	رَئِيس ٱلوُزَرَاء	ra'**ees** 'l-wuz**araa**'
secretary	سِكْرِتِير	sikri**teer**
treasurer	أَمِين ٱلصُّنْدُوق	'**ameen** '_s_-sun**dooq**

Phrases

The famous phrase below from the opening
Chapter of the Holy Quran is frequently placed
at the top of Arabic manuscripts:

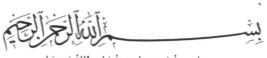

bismi 'lllaahi 'r-ra_h_mani 'r-ra_h_eem

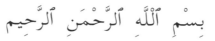

بِسْمِ ٱللَّهِ ٱلرَّحْمَنِ ٱلرَّحِيمِ

*In the Name of God (Allah) the Most Merciful
the Most Compassionate*

The Arabic below is typical of the message printed inside a greetings card sent to Muslims at the time of the two principal festivals in the Islamic calendar (the Eid Al-Fitr and Eid Al-Adha).

أَطْيَب ٱلْأَمَانِي وَأَسْعَد ٱلتَّهَانِي
بِمُنَاسَبَة ٱلْعِيد أَعَادَهُ ٱللَّهُ وَأَنْتُم
فِي صِحَّة وَرَخَاء وَهَنَاء وَعَافِيَة
وَكُلُّ عَامٍ وَأَنْتُم بِخَير

*' atyab 'l-' amaanee wa-' as^cad 't-tahaanee
bimunaasibat 'l-^ceed ' a^caadahu 'lllaahu wa-'antum
fee saha wa-rakhaa' wa-hanaa' wa-^caafeeya
wa-kullu ^caamin wa-antum bi-khayr.*

Greetings and best wishes on the occasion of the Eid festival

أَلرَّجَاء عَدَم ٱلتَّدْخِين

ar-rajaa' ʿadam at-tadkheen

Please do not smoke

مَمْنُوع ٱلدُّخُول

m a m n oo^c 'a d - d u kh oo l

Entry Forbidden

Bibliography

For further study of the script, language and culture of the Arab world:

A Dictionary of Modern Written Arabic, Arabic-English, Hans Wehr, *ed.* J Milton Cowan, Librairie du Liban, 1980.

Alif Baa - Introduction to Arabic Letters and Sounds, Kristen Brustad, Mahmoud Al-Batal, Abbas Al-Tonsi, Georgetown University Press, 1995.

Arabic - A complete course in reading and writing Arabic, Jack Smart and Frances Altorfer, Hodder Headline (Teach Yourself series), 2001.

Arabic Script, Gabriel Mandel Khan, Abbeville Press, 2001.

Beginner's Arabic Script - An introduction to reading and writing Arabic, John Mace, Hodder Headline (Teach Yourself series), 1999.

Mastering Arabic, Jane Wightwick and Mahmoud Gaafar, Palgrave, 1990.

Introduction to Modern Literary Arabic, David Cowan, Cambridge University Press, 1964.

The Arab World Handbook – Arabian Peninsula Edition, James Peters, Stacey International, 2000.

The Arabic Alphabet - How to read and write it, Nicholas Awde and Putros Samano, Saqi Books, 1986.

Very Simple Arabic - Incorporating Simple Etiquette in Arabia, James Peters, Stacey International, 2000.

Writing Arabic - A Practical Introduction to the Ruq'ah Script, T.F. Mitchell, Oxford University Press, 1953.

Notes